MICHAEL JACKSON

A Life from Beginning to End

Copyright © 2022 by Hourly History.

All rights reserved.

.

Table of Contents

Introduction

Michael Jackson came into this world on August 29, 1958, the son of Katherine and Joe Jackson. He began life in the old steel town of Gary, Indiana, about 25 miles (40 kilometers) southeast of Chicago. Named Michael Joseph Jackson, his middle name was gifted to him from his father Joe, whose rigid, authoritarian nature would become the backbone of Michael's early music career.

Michael came from a big family with nine children. His sisters were named Rebbie, La Toya, and Janet, and his brothers would come to include Jermaine, Marlon (Marlon also had a twin brother named Brandon who died soon after being born), Jackie, Tito, and Randy. It was with his brothers that Michael would first launch his singing career. Michael and his siblings inherited their musical talent directly from their parents; both Joe and Katherine were musically gifted, and as such, music was ever-present in the Jackson household.

It was while their father was at work that Michael and his brothers would sneak Joe's guitar out of the closet and try their luck at playing it.

Tito was the one who gravitated toward the instrument the most during these early years. According to family lore, one day he was strumming the strings just a bit too vigorously and accidentally broke one. He and his brothers were terrified. They knew that their father would be upset when he came home and found his guitar with a broken string, yet they didn't know how to put a new one on. In full panic, they put the guitar back in the closet and waited for the inevitable explosion.

Upon approaching Tito about the broken string, rather than punishing him, Joe asked Tito to show him what he had learned. When he saw the boy play, Joe wasn't mad—he was happy. He recognized his son's incredible potential with the instrument. Shortly thereafter, Joe came home with a brand-new guitar, handing the instrument over to Tito and telling him it was his. It was in this moment that the Jackson 5—and ultimately Michael Jackson's incredible solo career—began.

Chapter One

Early Life with the Jackson 5

"I would do my schooling which was three hours with a tutor and right after that I would go to the recording studio and record, and I'd record for hours and hours until it's time to go to sleep."

—Michael Jackson

Shortly after Michael's brother Tito was given his first guitar, the Jackson brothers began their first attempts at starting a band. Initially, Michael was mostly excluded since he was considered a bit too young by his older brothers at the time. His brothers would change their minds, however, after he performed a song for a talent contest at his elementary school and showed just how powerful of a singer he could be. Soon enough, Michael was practicing regularly with what would ultimately become the Jackson 5.

Michael and his brothers were dedicated to their craft, but it was their father Joe's dogged determination to make something of the group that really whipped them into shape. The phrase "whipped" might even be an adequate description since it would later be claimed that Joe Jackson wasn't above dishing out corporal punishment if his children failed to deliver musically. Michael later revealed that, on some occasions, he would get whipped by a belt if he didn't perform a song quite right.

At any rate, it was the stern guidance of Joe that helped the group rapidly evolve in their early days. It was also Joe who saved up whatever resources he had to buy the group musical equipment. After buying Tito his first guitar, he soon purchased a bass guitar, microphone, amps, and drums—all so his children could play. Joe, who himself was a musician, had a keen eye for talent, and even if he himself had missed the boat to superstardom, he developed a new determination to bring forth the best from his offspring.

It's said that Joe made sure that his sons practiced every single day after school. Although Michael loved music, he sometimes came to regret the fact that it was forced on him. He would later recall feeling envious of other kids who were able to go out and play after school while he and his brothers were obligated to stay inside for band practice.

Once the band had become a solid unit, Joe Jackson was ready to take them to the next level. He booked them for their first string of gigs at local talent shows and amateur hours in every venue he could find. The first break for the Jackson 5 came in 1966 when they managed to win a citywide competition at the high school Tito attended.

It was during these early performances that the boys first learned to connect with the audience and intersperse their music with carefully choreographed dance moves. Although they were young (Michael as only seven), they had become real crowd-pleasers. People liked what they saw and the Jackson kids were ready to give them more of it.

After being successful at talent shows like this, Joe Jackson had his sons perform at some less-than-stellar nightclubs such as Mr. Lucky's Lounge in Gary, Indiana. These joints not only served booze but also frequently had strippers working the venue. Obviously, such a place would not have been an appropriate environment in which minors like the Jacksons should have been performing. Nevertheless, Joe was determined to have his children perform in front of as many live audiences as they could, no matter how seedy the venue might have been.

The next big break for the Jacksons came when Joe connected with a co-worker of his who happened to have access to a recording studio. It was through this contact that the Jackson 5 recorded their first song, "Big Boy." Recorded and released in 1967, the song didn't get much traction outside of Gary, but it was an exciting moment for the Jacksons all the same. For them, it was amazing just to hear their music preserved on a record.

Joe knew full well, however, that if the Jackson 5 were ever going to hit it big, they needed to make their presence known outside of their hometown. This led him to pack up his sons and their equipment and make the drive to Chicago, where they performed at an amateur night at Chicago's Royal George Theatre. Here, the Jackson 5 proved that they were as good as gold when they delivered a flawless performance and won the competition.

Over the next few weeks, they continued to win, and eventually, they were rewarded with the privilege of being able to open a show with none other than the superstars Gladys Knight and the Pips. Both the audience and Gladys were impressed with how well the Jackson 5 did, and shortly after the show, Gladys had a personal, one-on-one discussion with Joe Jackson, during which she expressed to him how she wished to aid him in promoting the band.

Gladys had connections and let Joe know that she was going to tell the owner of Motown Records—Berry Gordy, Jr.—just how impressed she was. Motown Records was founded in Detroit, Michigan, and was called as such due to the long-standing nickname of Detroit, "Motor City." Since Motown had opened its doors in 1959, it had become a prominent staple of the music scene. Motor City was Motown, and Motown was Motor City.

Joe Jackson was hopeful that Gladys Knight could generate some interest for the group with Motown's Berry Gordy. At the same time, he was also going to make sure that he did everything within his power to streamline the process. Soon, the Jackson 5 were making the four-hour drive to Detroit in order to perform in the Motor City for themselves. Their next big gig, however, wouldn't be in Chicago or Detroit, but rather New York City.

On August 13, 1967, the Jackson 5 went all the way to New York to perform at the famed Apollo Theatre. Fortunately for Joe, the big wigs at the Apollo had already heard of the band and were so impressed with what people were saying that they were automatically entered into the amateur finals without even having to audition. Those running the show at the Apollo would not be disappointed. The Jackson 5 proved to be the best act that night and came in first place.

Although the Jacksons were thrilled with their progress, they knew that without a big-time record company backing them, they wouldn't be able to break out to a larger audience. Fortunately, shortly thereafter, the Jackson brothers were made aware that their golden opportunity had arrived; Joe sat the boys down to tell them that Motown Records had finally come calling.

Chapter Two

Rise to Stardom

"I had pimples so badly it used to make me so shy. . . . I wouldn't want to look in the mirror and my father teased me and I just hated it and I cried every day."

—Michael Jackson

Michael Jackson was only ten years old when he and his brothers auditioned for Motown. The group collectively took a deep breath, put forward their best material, and gave it their all. As was customary at the time, the studio personnel who took it all in made sure that they kept their thoughts to themselves. After politely thanking the boys for their performance, they simply told them that they "would be in touch."

The suspense was almost too much for the Jacksons to bear, but fortunately, they didn't have to wait very long. In just a matter of days, they were contacted and asked to pay another visit to Motown. It was during this next tour of the studio that they would be greeted by none other than Berry Gordy. Gordy didn't pull any punches and promptly informed the Jackson 5 that he intended to make them "very famous."

The first song released by the group under the Motown label was the 1969 hit "I Want You Back." After the success of this single, Gordy—with the aid of his top performer Diana Ross—crafted the first feature-length Jackson 5 album, which was simply called *Diana Ross Presents the Jackson 5*. This album was just as successful as its first single.

It was after their career began to really take off in this way that Berry Gordy convinced the Jackson family to make the move to Los Angeles, California. LA was—and still is—a place of great opportunity for performers, and it also had a satellite office for Motown at the time.

Shortly after their arrival in Los Angeles, the Jackson 5 made their debut on *The Ed Sullivan Show*. This was a classic variety show that had hosted several well-known breakthrough acts. Both Elvis and the Beatles were launched into the stratosphere after appearing on this platform, and now it was the Jackson 5's turn. They did indeed become a rapid success story, as youngsters all over the country began to idolize the group. Soon after appearing on *Ed Sullivan*, their faces were being plastered on posters, magazine covers, and various other merchandise. They even made an appearance in cartoon form for a Saturday morning cartoon on ABC called *The Jackson 5ive*.

The group had already achieved superstardom in their own right, but by the time Michael reached the age of 13, he made it clear that he was ready to try his luck on his own. Michael first embarked upon his solo career in 1972, with the release of the solo record *Got to Be There*. This was followed by another album called *Ben*. The second album proved to be even more successful than the first solo record, scoring Michael a hit with the title track "Ben," which was a tune that was dedicated to his pet rat of the same name. Yes, young Michael did indeed have an eclectic taste when it came to pets, and ever since his Gary days, he had been fond of pet rats.

During this time, Michael also continued to contribute to the Jackson 5 and would go on to finish up the next studio album with them, entitled *Lookin' Through the Windows*, which hit store shelves in the summer of 1972. This was then followed by Michael's next solo album, *Music & Me*. Michael was going through the natural changes of adolescence at this time, which came with a bad case of acne. This is a normal phase for all teenagers, but since Michael was in the spotlight so much, it was devastating for him.

Nevertheless, he persevered, and by the fall of 1973, Michael was impressing the audience of the variety show *Soul Train* with his moves for the Jackson 5's new epic, "Dancing Machine." In the song, Michael innovated a new robotic-styled dance in which he danced along in short, mechanical movements. Jackson meanwhile continued to work on his solo recordings, continuing to perfect his craft.

The Jackson 5 would release what would be their last album for Motown in the summer of 1975 with the record *Moving Violation*. Due to artistic disagreement, the band had decided it was time to move on to another record label. They were no longer able to use the name Jackson 5 since it had become a trademark of Motown. Instead, they returned to their old name of just the Jacksons. The group would then release a well-received album called *Destiny* in 1978. This record featured the hit song "Blame It on the Boogie."

Along with all of these developments, it was that same year that Michael made his acting debut on the production of *The Wiz*, which was a reproduction of the classic Wizard of Oz story, starring none other than Diana Ross. It was while Michael was being cast alongside Diana Ross for *The Wiz* that he became acquainted with the highly skilled record producer Quincy Jones.

With Quincy Jones, Jackson would make what would be his most successful solo album up to that point—the disco heavy *Off the Wall*. This album, although eventually outdone by *Thriller*, would give Michael the first few hits of his adult career. He was around 20 years old at the time and could be proud of the success of killer tracks such as "Rock with You" and "Don't Stop 'Til You Get Enough."

Still, for Michael Jackson, this wasn't quite enough. Although *Off the Wall* was successful, Michael craved more, and just like his hit song proclaimed, he wasn't going to stop until he got it. Shortly thereafter, he was back to the studio, redoubling his efforts for what would ultimately become his epic masterpiece, *Thriller*.

Chapter Three

The Golden Years: Thriller

"It wasn't easy to get the family to this point. I had to work two jobs. I had all nine kids. I stayed there with them and got them all into show biz. I don't care what anyone else said, I did my job."

—Joe Jackson

Michael Jackson and Quincy Jones put their heads together in the early 1980s and came up with a masterpiece. After many hours of studio time, the blockbuster album *Thriller* was released in November of 1982. This album would be the greatest Michael Jackson record of all time, producing a total of seven hit songs. Tracks like "Thriller" and "Billie Jean" would become not only hits but cultural markers of the 1980s as a whole.

After the critical success of his latest album, Jackson further cemented his place in history when he made an appearance in 1983 on a televised celebration of Motown records, called *Motown 25: Yesterday, Today, Forever*. He rejoined the Jackson 5 to perform some of their classics, but Michael was the showstopper when he performed solo. The most memorable moment of the whole affair was when he performed "Billie Jean."

During the song, Jackson introduced a new dance move which has since been dubbed the moonwalk. It consisted of Michael gliding backward as he simultaneously seemed to be making forward-walking motions. The move is essentially a kind of fake-out routine, in which one is sliding backward while pretending to move forward with the rest of their body. It's a rather simple concept, yet the way Jackson did it, the move seemed so convincing it almost seemed like magic.

Michael Jackson was already rising to the top with *Thriller*, but this cameo broadcast on NBC in 1983 sent him hurtling through the stratosphere to even higher heights of fame. Interestingly enough, Jackson had initially considered declining the invitation to perform; it was only when Motown's Berry Gordy insisted that he show up and also promised the opportunity for a solo performance that Michael finally agreed.

Due to all of the major accolades that were being hurled Jackson's way, by the time of the 26th Annual Grammy Awards in 1984, he was managed to win a record-breaking eight awards for *Thriller*, as well as an additional award for his work on the audiobook version of *E.T. the Extraterrestrial*.

Michael Jackson was already rich and famous, but in 1985, he also proved himself to be a savvy businessman when he purchased the copyrights of the Beatles music catalog. It cost him some 47 million dollars, but it would prove to be a highly lucrative asset for Jackson in later years. During this period, Jackson had also begun to show an interest in various social causes. In 1984, he allowed "Beat It" to be used for a PSA warning of the dangers of drunk driving. For his efforts, he was awarded the Presidential Humanitarian Award by then-President Ronald Reagan.

Being awarded a humanitarian award seemed to set the stage for one of Michael's greatest humanitarian efforts. In 1985, big wigs in the music business were alerted to the widespread famine that was taking place in the East African nation of Ethiopia. The idea of holding massive benefit concerts was conceived, and for this cause, Jackson helped write and record the mega-hit song, "We Are the World," which would be the theme song of the entire effort.

The recording was a monumental production that had a number of famous artists making cameo appearances on the track. The song itself managed to raise some 60 million dollars for the cause. Jackson got three Grammys for his efforts, and the song also made history as the first to go multiplatinum.

Despite all of his good works, by the mid-1980s, Jackson was beginning to get what would be a long tradition of bad press. Gossip columns noting his seeming change in appearance, coupled with his eccentric lifestyle, began to make Jackson a number one topic of sensational tabloid stories. Michael Jackson would later admit that he did undergo some plastic surgery and that he had undertaken certain cosmetic measures for his skin due to the onset of the hereditary skin disease vitiligo. This skin condition leaves those suffering from it with an uneven complexion due to a loss of pigment in various patches of their skin. Jackson initially tried to cover up the effects of this illness with makeup, but according to some sources, he eventually opted to use some lightener to even out his skin tone.

It was this sense of being hunted by the media that led Jackson to write one of his next big hits, "Leave Me Alone." Known as a kind of "paranoid anthem" for its frantic energy as Michael shouts out his need for escape from his imagined pursuers, the song captures Michael at his very best. Just like "Billie Jean," this track has Jackson on the run as he exercises all of his demons to a driving and catchy beat.

"Leave Me Alone" was recorded for Jackson's 1987 *Bad* album. Michael Jackson would shatter expectations once again with this record, featuring not just one but five No. 1 singles. Immediately after the album's release, Jackson embarked upon a world tour that would have him crisscrossing the globe from September of 1987 to January of 1989. This was Jackson's first-ever solo world tour. Finally getting out from under the shadow of the Jackson 5, it would be the first of many.

Michael Jackson was a very rich man by the late 1980s, and in 1988, he made a major acquisition. He bought up some 2,700 acres of ranch land in California, which he dubbed Neverland Ranch. It was here that Jackson would build his dream home. Much more than a mere dream home, Neverland—like its name might imply—became an entrance into Michael's own personal fairy tale world.

The ranch was named after the mythical home of Peter Pan. Peter Pan was a character known for his inability to grow up, and he was, in many ways, a figure with whom Michael Jackson could personally identify and relate. Like Peter Pan, he often felt as if he was never really allowed to grow up and had remained a child. Many have since theorized that Jackson was so child-like because he never got to have a normal childhood due to nonstop performances from an early age.

So it was that Michael Jackson created his own Neverland in which he could relax and recreate the childhood he never had. Here, he would pull out all the stops, installing amusement park rides, swimming pools, a movie theater, and a zoo. Jackson even had his own train, which traveled around on railroad tracks that stretched across the compound.

As well as using it as his own personal playground, Michael began to make use of Neverland as a resort for underprivileged and sick children. It was meant to be a place where they could relax and forget about their troubles. At first, Jackson was commended for his charity; it all seemed in line with his recent philanthropic efforts. Most were proud of his work. Then, scandal and accusations of the worst kind ground the trains and amusement park rides of Neverland to a screeching halt.

Chapter Four

Betrayal at Neverland

"When I see children, I see the face of God.
That's why I love them so much."

—Michael Jackson

Despite Michael Jackson's immense success in the music industry, he regularly courted controversy with the press. He was constantly questioned over his changing appearance, childlike behavior, and even over rumors that he wished to purchase the Elephant Man's bones. Even though all the press about his eccentricities bothered him, by the dawning of the 1990s, Jackson was trying to ignore all the chatter and focus on the making of his new album.

Released in the fall of 1991, Michael Jackson's next masterpiece would be entitled *Dangerous*. Upon its release, the album immediately shot to number one on the charts. One of the album's hits and most memorable tracks was the socially conscious piece "Black or

White." In this song, Jackson delivers a simple yet powerful plea for racial harmony in which the chorus reassures the listener in several variations, "If you're thinkin' of being my baby—it don't matter if you're black or white. I said if you're thinkin' of being my brother—it don't matter if you're black or white."

The accompanying music video was also one of Jackson's most memorable. In it, people were depicted morphing not only from one ethnicity to another but also from one gender to another, in a manner that seemed to simultaneously celebrate and render meaningless entrenched concepts of human identity.

It was around the time of the release of *Dangerous* that Michael Jackson began greater outreach to the underprivileged, needy, and those suffering from debilitating illnesses by creating his Heal the World Foundation. This foundation had the mission of raising money for children in need and also allowed them to sign on for visits and even extended stays at Neverland Ranch. Demonstrating just how dedicated he was to this cause, Jackson would end up donating all of his proceeds from the Dangerous World Tour to his newly established foundation. Trouble would come, however, when one of the boys who had stayed at Neverland accused the star of molesting him.

It was in August of 1993 that Jordan Chandler, who was only 13 at the time, leveled the shocking accusations. Chandler claimed that Jackson had kissed him and engaged in oral sex and masturbatory acts with him. Michael, for his part, immediately denied the charges and claimed that it was all an extortion campaign engineered by the boy's father, Evan Chandler. Nevertheless, authorities took the charges very seriously and conducted a raid of Jackson's home shortly thereafter.

The raid found little in the way of incriminating evidence, but investigators did discover some questionable artifacts. Among them was a book that featured boys playing and swimming in various states of undress. The book, although raising much suspicion, was not in itself considered illegal.

Seeking more conclusive evidence, investigators asked Jackson's accuser what his genitalia looked like. Fortunately for Jackson, his accuser's description did not seem to match up with the facts. In order for his interrogators to figure all of this out, Jackson had to be strip-searched and physically inspected. Despite this humiliation, when it was all said and done, it seemed that the facts were on Jackson's side. Still, apparently not willing to risk a guilty verdict, Jackson went ahead and settled with his accuser outside of court, handing over some 25 million dollars to make the charges go away.

The fact that Michael Jackson paid off his accuser only increased public suspicions. Many wondered why he would agree to pay an accuser off; if he were indeed innocent, such actions would only seem to invite others to level false accusations against him. Those that knew Jackson, however, contended that he simply didn't have the stomach for a long, drawn-out court battle. In addition, Jackson was by this point battling an addiction to painkillers, which he had turned to in order to cope with the stress over the allegations.

It seems that, whichever way you look at it, a great betrayal had taken place at Neverland. If Michael Jackson was telling the truth, his trust had been betrayed by those who he only wished to help. If, on the other hand, the child and his family were being truthful, it was their trust that had been horribly betrayed. It's still unclear what really happened at Neverland Ranch.

Chapter Five

Marriage to Lisa Maria Presley

"I will never stop helping and loving people the way Jesus said to."

—Michael Jackson

Michael Jackson was one of the biggest stars in the world in the early 1990s, but the accusations of child molestation in 1993 had a severe impact on his public image. His blockbuster album *Dangerous* was suddenly overshadowed by these very serious charges. Even when the case against him was cast aside, the media ceaselessly followed every lurid detail of the ordeal.

Close on the heels of this drama, Jackson would generate even more media attention when he made it known his intention to marry Lisa Marie Presley, the daughter of rock icon Elvis Presley. Most had no idea that Michael even knew Lisa Marie, but the truth was they had a relationship that went back a number of years. They had first met in 1974 after a performance of the Jackson 5 and remained friends through the years.

Their relationship had naturally evolved over time, leading up to Jackson's marriage proposal in late 1993. Although this was a completely natural process, because it coincided so closely with the child molestation scandal, many were under the impression that it was nothing more than some kind of publicity stunt to distract the public from what Jackson had been so recently accused of. Lisa Marie, for one, denied this theory and famously stated at the time, "I'm not gonna marry somebody for any reason other than the fact that I've fallen in love with them."

One person who seemed utterly convinced that Michael Jackson and Lisa Marie Presley were truly in love was real estate mogul—and eventual president of the United States—Donald J. Trump. Trump and Jackson had been friends for some time, and after he married Lisa Marie, the married couple frequently stayed at Trump's Mar-a-Lago resort in Florida, as well as the famous Trump Tower in New York. Trump told *People Magazine* in 1994 that he had witnessed the two "holding hands and talking into the wee hours."

He was apparently convinced that their love for each other was real.

At any rate, Lisa Marie and Michael Jackson were lawfully wed in May of 1994 while they were vacationing in La Vega in the Dominican Republic. That fall, the couple made an appearance at the MTV Video Music Awards. Standing close together, Jackson announced, "Welcome to the MTV Music Awards. I'm very happy to be here." He then looked over to Lisa Marie and remarked, "Just think, nobody thought this would last." After he spoke those words, he and Lisa Marie shared a passionate (although some would say somewhat awkward) kiss.

Despite the show they put on, the couple's marriage would end in divorce after less than two years. In the meantime, Jackson would launch his next great musical endeavor, the double album *HIStory*. The first disc of the *HIStory* album is a greatest hits compilation, featuring some of the best tracks that Jackson had come up with to date. The second disc is a riveting and emotional journey through Jackson's most recent turmoil. Here, you find painful and raw songs such as "They Don't Really Care About Us." Although this is an angry track, it's catchy with an infectious beat as Jackson lyrically vents his frustration about the injustices he sees afoot in the world.

According to Jackson, the song was meant to be a stand against injustice and discrimination, but due to his choice of lyrics, some viewed the song as offensive and discriminatory. The lyrics in question still remain highly controversial, so it's perhaps best to let the reader interpret the meaning for themselves. The lyrics that were found the most troubling were the lines, "Beat me, hate me, you can never break me / Will me, thrill me, you can never kill me / Jew me, sue me, everybody do me / Kick me, kike me, don't you black or white me." These words were then followed by the captivating chorus, "All I wanna say is that they don't really care about us."

Although Jackson has long maintained that his motivations for writing this song have been misinterpreted, he was condemned for anti-Semitism for the lines "Jew me, sue me" and "kick me, kike me." Jackson claimed that he was criticizing those that would use such words and expressing his own feelings of victimization through them, but others didn't see it that way and demanded that he change the lyrics. Jackson ultimately apologized and agreed to change the lyrics. Later recordings changed the words to "do me, sue me" and "kick me, strike me."

Besides such hard-driving tracks, Jackson also revealed a soft and vulnerable side with the smash hit, "You Are Not Alone." This song broke records when it became the first single to make its debut in the number one slot on the *Billboard* chart. Despite his troubles, this hit proved that Michael Jackson was still able to dominate the charts. His frenetic pace would come to a halt in late 1995, however, when he suddenly collapsed due to a panic attack while prepping for a gig on a TV program.

HIStory would be Michael's last best-selling album, and in many ways, it would mark his last hurrah as a hit-making machine in the music industry. It was an inflection point in Jackson's musical career immediately before a long, slow decline.

Chapter Six

Jackson's Children

"Everyone who knows me will know the truth, which is that my children come first in my life."

—Michael Jackson

Jackson was on tour for his *HIStory* album from September 7, 1996, to October 15, 1997. During this time, he put on 82 shows across 35 different countries. It was while Jackson was on the Australian leg of the tour that he quietly married a woman named Debbie Rowe. No one would have guessed Jackson would get married so soon after divorcing Lisa Marie Presley, but as it turned out, Debbie was already pregnant with Michael's baby. Michael Jackson was almost 40 years old at this point and had never much talked about having children of his own. The prospect that he would finally become a father took many by surprise.

Michael had first met Debbie Rowe some 15 years prior when Michael was undergoing treatment at a dermatology clinic for his chronic vitiligo. Debbie was a nurse at the facility and worked as an assistant to Michael's dermatology doctor, Arnold Klein. Debbie, a lady with a good sense of humor, was able to break the ice with Jackson early on. According to her, their first few words together consisted of the following, "I go 'Hi,' and he goes 'Hi,' and I said, 'You know what? Nobody does what you do better, and nobody does what I do better. Let's get this over with.'" Debbie recalled that her famous patient then burst into laughter; they were friends ever since.

Michael and Debbie became reacquainted shortly after his divorce from Lisa Marie. Debbie would later recount how Michael opened up to her about how lonely he felt in the aftermath of his divorce, and Debbie stepped into the role as his comforter. Not only that—when Jackson expressed to her his desire to have children, she readily volunteered to assist him in the enterprise. This is the part of the story that is still controversial, but after Michael's death, Debbie claimed that she and Michael never had sex and that the two children she supplied him with came by way of artificial insemination.

According to Debbie Rowe, the source of the sperm she received is unknown, but some have alleged that the donor may actually have been Debbie's former supervisor, Arnold Klein. Klein, who has since passed away, admitted to submitting a donation to the sperm bank, but he always maintained that he did not know if he was the father or not. In 2009, he went on the record to state, "I still can't answer absolutely one way or another. I once donated to the sperm bank. To the best of my knowledge, I am not the father."

Jackson's now-grown-up kids have also long grappled with the question of who their biological father actually is, but it was perhaps Michael's son Prince who put it best when he mused, "Every time someone asks me that, I ask, 'What's the point? What difference does it make?'" For Jackson's children, he will always be their father whether he is biologically related to them or not.

At any rate, Debbie Rowe gave birth to the child who would be Michael's first-born son, Michael Joseph Jackson, Jr. (also known as Prince) on February 13, 1997. Rowe would then go on to give birth to a daughter, Paris Katherine Jackson, on April 3, 1998. Jackson was indeed eager to be a father. In a later interview, he relayed the shocking story of how he was so exceedingly excited at the birth of Paris that he didn't even wait for her to be cleaned up before he took her home, afterbirth and all.

Michael Jackson and Debbie Rowe would then go on to divorce in 1999. Rowe, standing by her pledge to give Michael the children he desired, agreed to give Michael full custody of the children. Rowe would later explain her decision by stating, "I did it for him to become a father, not for me to become a mother. You earn the title parent. I have done absolutely nothing to earn that title." Rowe would also get eight million dollars in the divorce settlement and a house in Beverly Hills.

While raising his first two children, Jackson was also busy putting together a remix album called *Blood on the Dance Floor: HIStory in the Mix*. Along with remixed tracks from the *HIStory* album, the record also had five new songs. This album was not very well received in the United States, but interestingly enough, it did well outside of America. Such things caused many to speculate that the reason why the record was lagging behind in the United States was not so much due to the quality of the music, as it was Michael's increasingly negative reputation among Americans.

Although Michael Jackson would receive a kind of revival in the minds of many Americans after his death, his public reputation had hit an all-time low during the late 1990s and early 2000s. It was a frustrating period for Jackson because he knew that he could still make good songs. Still, the negative press that hung over everything he did constantly threatened to derail his work. Soon, one carefully crafted journalistic hit piece would threaten to end his career for good.

Chapter Seven

Court Battles and Controversies

"Why can't you share your bed? The most loving thing to do is to share your bed with someone. It's very charming. It's very sweet. It's what the whole world should do."

—Michael Jackson

Michael Jackson would release his final full album in the fall of 2001. With the name *Invincible*, Jackson was obviously attempting to project strength and reassert himself with this record. He had been through a lot, and this was meant to be his comeback album that would once again cement his place on the top.

Thanks to his efforts, Jackson did manage to squeeze out one single that broke into the top ten—the grooving "You Rock My World"—but beyond the fleeting success of this one track and continued success overseas, the album did not perform as well in the United States. Jackson blamed part of the reason for this on the head of his record label, Sony's Tommy Mottola.

After completing the album, Jackson had announced that he would not be renewing his contract, which supposedly made Tommy Mottola decide to cut back promotion for an artist that was ready to jump ship. Jackson, angered by the move, went public with his displeasure. At an epic press conference, he memorably condemned Mottola, stating that "He's mean, he's a racist, and he's very, very, very devilish."

No one seemed to take Jacksons' claims too seriously at the time, and beyond generating a brief spectacle, the remarks did not seem to accomplish much. It even earned a rebuke from civil rights activist Al Sharpton who happened to be on good terms with Mottola. Sharpton went on the record to state, "I have known Tommy for 15 or 20 years, and never once have I known him to say or do anything that would be considered racist."

After Sharpton's remarks, much of the wind went out of the sails of Jackson's accusations against Mottola. Sony then doubled down and defended Mottola, condemning Jackson's actions. Sony issued an official response that read in part,

"We were deeply offended by the outrageous comments Mr. Jackson made during his publicity stunt this past Saturday. The executive he attacked is widely supported and respected in every part of the music industry and has championed both Mr. Jackson's career and the careers of many other superstars."

Jackson was fighting a losing battle when it came to taking on Sony, and he inevitably became disillusioned and disappointed with the results. In reality, *Invincible* did well enough, but Jackson wanted it to be one of his greatest works to date. Whatever the contributing factors may have been, it just didn't reach the same level as previous Michael Jackson albums.

After *Invincible*, Jackson would take an extended break from music. He began to spend more time with his children, and in 2002, he had a woman—whose identity has never been revealed—serve as a surrogate to give birth to what would be his third child. Jackson named this child similarly to his first, his proper name being Prince Michael Jackson II. He would, however, become much better known by the nickname his father gave him, "Blanket." Michael is said to have called his son this because a blanket represents warmth and love. Whatever the case may be, the name stuck, and Jackson would call his youngest child Blanket for the rest of his life.

It was with Blanket that Michael would generate his next round of bad publicity, when shortly after the child was born, an overexcited Jackson held the boy over the balcony of the hotel he was staying at so that a crowd of fans down below could see him. The media picked up the startling images of the proud dad dangling the child in mid-air for a few precarious seconds.

The move was certainly dangerous. Jackson's hotel room was four stories up, and just one slip of Michael's grip would have meant certain death for Blanket. Soon enough, the image of Michael Jackson dangling his child over a balcony was on the front cover of all the tabloids. Michael himself was later horrified by his own actions and issued an official apology for what he expressed as bad judgment on his part.

Just as the bad publicity of this incident was dying down, British journalist Martin Bashir came into contact with Michael Jackson and arranged for a series of interviews to be made. Bashir began documenting Jackson's personal life in the summer of 2002. The singer hoped that the documentary would help him set the record straight about his personal life, but it backfired in the worst way possible.

The most controversial moment of the piece was when Jackson was shown holding hands with a little boy who stayed at the ranch while he discussed the sleeping arrangements at Neverland. Jackson maintained that there was nothing wrong with a grown man sleeping in the same bed as a child. At one point during the taping, while his guest leaned his head on Michael's shoulder, he even declared, "The most loving thing to do is share your bed with someone."

The jury is still out on whether or not any of the suspicions against Michael Jackson are true, and opinions on the subject seem to fall into camps. Some believe that Jackson's constant eyebrow-raising behavior in this regard confirms that he did indeed have an attraction to children. Others insist that Michael Jackson was a deeply misunderstood man and that he, in many ways childlike himself, merely related to children and loved them in a completely benign way.

As soon as the final production of the piece, which was called *Living with Michael Jackson*, aired in February of 2003, the general public was shocked by what they saw. Here, they found

Michael Jackson—a man who had already been accused of inappropriate conduct with minors—openly admitting to hosting sleepovers and on some occasions even sharing his bed with children.

It was this controversial TV appearance that sparked a renewed suspicion of Jackson's activities, and shortly thereafter, a child once again accused the pop star of the unthinkable. The singer was hit with seven counts of child molestation as well as two counts of intoxicating a minor with alcoholic drinks. His accuser claimed that Jackson had plied kids with wine, which Jackson supposedly referred to as "Jesus juice." Despite all of these claims, however, once the case went to trial in 2005, no substantial evidence was found that any crime had been committed. Jackson was ultimately found not guilty.

According to those that knew Michael Jackson best, this second round of accusations was absolutely devastating for him, and he never really recovered. Even over a decade after his passing, these accusations continue to haunt Michael Jackson to this very day.

Chapter Eight

Hiding in Bahrain

"I'm never pleased with anything. I'm a perfectionist. It's part of who I am."

—Michael Jackson

After his latest round of legal trouble was put behind him, Jackson and his three children relocated for a time to the Persian Gulf, where they stayed in Bahrain at the behest of Michael's friend, Sheikh Abdullah, the son of the king of Bahrain. His friend, being a member of the Bahraini royal family, was indeed a powerful benefactor.

Besides being a Michael Jackson fan, Abdullah was also an avid musician. He became convinced that he could be a part of Michael's next blockbuster music endeavor, announcing to the press at the time that he was absolutely certain that they would have a song created in Bahrain which would "show the world that this region is not about wars and conflicts."

Jackson's stay in the Persian Gulf would be mired in bad public relations once again when he was allegedly caught inside a women's bathroom at Dubai's famed Ibn Battuta Mall. Jackson later claimed that the whole thing was an accident, but due to the conservative tendencies of the region, such things were not taken lightly. According to Randall Sullivan's book *Untouchable*, Jackson, who often wore disguises, had used the rather convenient one considering the circumstances of covering his face with a veil and wearing a black, full-length gown that was worn by local Muslim women in the region.

Covered up in this outfit, no one knew he was Michael Jackson, but it was apparently while so covered that he accidentally stepped into the women's bathroom. Whether it was an accident or not, in the religiously conservative United Arab Emirates, if Jackson stepped into a men's room dressed as a woman or into a women's room as a man, it was bound to get attention.

According to Randall Sullivan, an alarmed woman exiting from a toilet stall squealed in horror at the sight of Jackson's "mangled face." Michael was supposedly applying makeup when confronted by the woman. This alleged encounter made its way to all the local papers the next day, and soon, it was circulating in the international press as well.

Locals quickly turned on Jackson, and some even demanded that he be punished for his actions. As good of a friend as Sheikh Abdullah was to Jackson, it seems that even he had to cave under the pressure. Shortly thereafter, he informed Michael that he would have to leave his residence.

The Sheikh put Michael up in nearby Oman instead, where the singer stayed at the Al Bustan Palace hotel. The stay was a brief one, and by 2006, Jackson had traveled all the way to Ireland, where he had begun work at a recording studio in the region of County Westmeath. Although these sessions did not amount to much during his lifetime, Jackson famously allowed journalists from *Access Hollywood* to document his time in the studio. In the interview, Jackson, who had always found Ireland's mythic history enchanting, happily declared, "Ireland has inspired me to make a great album. I have never given up on making music."

Jackson would leave Ireland for the U.S. by the end of the year when he heard the news that his good friend and mentor James Brown had passed away. James Brown had been a great influence on Michael's music from the beginning, and despite his trepidation of returning stateside, Jackson was determined to pay his respects. At Brown's funeral, he issued a heartfelt statement, telling those in attendance, "Ever since I was a small child—no more than six years old—my mother would wake me no matter what time it was, to watch the television to see the master at work. Every time I saw him move; I was mesmerized. I've never seen a performer like J. B. and right then and there, I knew that was exactly what I wanted to do with my life. James Brown, I shall miss you and I love you so much. Thank you for everything."

After this public appearance for James Brown's funeral, Jackson would mostly keep a low profile for the next few years. He was so far under the radar at this point that he was almost forgotten. As such, it came as a surprise when he announced that he would launch a brand-new concert tour which he referred to as his "final curtain call." For all who were interested, Michael Jackson let it be known that the stage had been set—and this was his last act.

Chapter Nine

Late Life and Death

"They always say, 'Time heals.' But it really doesn't. You just get used to it."

—Paris Jackson

In the spring of 2009, it was announced that Michael Jackson would launch the This Is It farewell concert series that would be kicked off at O2 Arena in London, England, before moving further afield to various other locations between July 13, 2009, and March 6, 2010.

In the lead-up to the planned concerts, Jackson's publicity machine was in overdrive. Michael had a lot riding on the performances, and he wanted to generate a large buzz for them. Not only was he depending upon the gigs to re-establish his legacy, but he was also very much in need of the revenue that the concerts would provide. Jackson's finances were strained at this stage in his life, and Neverland Ranch was actually on the verge of going into foreclosure. It was the proceeds from the This Is It concert series that Jackson hoped would rescue his ailing assets.

Jackson held a press conference in promotion of the tour in which he outlined how he would perform shows in London before moving on to Paris, New York, and eventually Mumbai. Jackson furthermore made it clear that he planned to go into retirement upon the conclusion of the concerts. Such a proclamation helped boost ticket sales since diehard fans were now under the impression that if they wanted to see their idol in the flesh, it was now or never—this was it. Ticket sales were good, and promoters were quite excited for their prospects for profit, pinning all of their hopes on Michael Jackson. The pressure was now on, and Jackson wanted to be at his best.

Back home in California, he rigorously practiced for several hours at a time, making sure that his routine was absolutely perfect. On June 24, 2009, he showed up at the Staples Center in Los Angeles, where he participated in a routine rehearsal with fellow performers who would share the stage with him. By all accounts, Jackson was in great spirits, and he was doing a good job on all of the practiced routines. The next day, however, tragedy would strike.

On June 25, Michael Jackson was found unconscious and unable to breathe. One of Jackson's personal doctors, Conrad Murray, was present at the time and was immediately summoned to aid the ailing star. Sadly enough, Murray's efforts failed to resuscitate Jackson. An ambulance was eventually called, and Jackson was picked up and taken to UCLA Medical Center. Again, attempts were made to bring life back into the singer's cold, lifeless form, but again, the efforts were not successful. Michael Jackson, aged 50, was already gone.

It was only in the aftermath of Jackson's sudden death that it would come to light that his physician, Conrad Murray, had been giving him routine doses of a powerful sedative called propofol along with other downers such as lorazepam and midazolam. An autopsy would confirm that Jackson's ultimate cause of death was a massive overdose of the drug propofol.

Michael Jackson was, of course, the one who had requested the drugs, but in light of his death, blame would be shifted to the one who prescribed them, Conrad Murray. Murray would be deemed negligent in his duties as a physician and would ultimately be found guilty of involuntary manslaughter in the wake of Jackson's death. He would spend two years behind bars as a result. No matter who was to blame, nothing could bring the King of Pop back.

Conclusion

The world was shocked to learn of Michael Jackson's death. It was particularly shocking because he perished right before he was scheduled to launch his super-hyped farewell tour. Instead of fans getting to see Jackson perform one last time, it was announced that a memorial service would be held for the King of Pop at the Staples Center in Los Angeles.

It's said that an incredible one and a half million attempted to gain entrance to the memorial services, and of these less than eighteen thousand were randomly selected. Jackson's funeral was a concert in itself, with famous performers such as Stevie Wonder, Lionel Richie, and Mariah Carey taking the stage. Even John Mayer was there to perform a moving rendition of "Human Nature" on guitar.

Many who knew Michael Jackson also spoke on behalf of their old friend, seeking to set the record straight about a man they felt that the world had long misunderstood. Al Sharpton, in particular, wished to explore this phenomenon, at one point directing his message to Michael's children. He told them, "Wasn't nothing strange about your daddy. It was strange what your daddy had to deal with. But he dealt with it anyway."

In the end, it was Jackson's kids themselves who stole the show. This was the first time that the world had really gotten to know Michael Jackson's children since he had purposely tried to keep them from the limelight. By the time 11-year-old Paris Jackson stood on stage to speak of the man whom she loved more than life itself, the whole world's heart seemed to break. As much as Michael Jackson had been hunted and hounded for his flaws and controversies, it was through the tears of his children that many began to see him in a new light. His children were absolutely distraught at the loss of their father, and in the expression of their grief, they reminded the world of how they, too, had once loved the King of Pop, Michael Jackson.

Bibliography

Campbell, Lisa (1993). *Michael Jackson: The King of Pop.*

Jackson, Michael (1998). *Moonwalk.*

Lewis Jones, Jel D. (2005). *Michael Jackson, the King of Pop: The Big Picture: the Music! the Man! the Legend! the Interviews: an Anthology.*

Knopper, Steve (2016). *MJ: The Genius of Michael Jackson.*

Mansour, David (2005). *From Abba to Zoom: A Pop Culture Encyclopedia of the Late 20th Century.*

Sullivan, Randall (2012). *Untouchable: The Strange Life and Tragic Death of Michael Jackson.*

Taraborrelli, J. Randy (1991). *Michael Jackson: The Magic and the Madness.*

Vogel, Joseph (2012). *Man in the Music: The Creative Life and Work of Michael Jackson.*